www.clfpublishing.org
909.315.3161

Copyright © 2020 by Cassundra White-Elliott.

All rights reserved. No portion of this book may be reproduced, stored in a retrieval system, or transmitted by any form or any means electronically, photocopied, recorded, or any other except for brief quotations in printed reviews, without the prior permission of the publisher.

Cover design by Senir Design. Contact info: info@senirdesign.com

ISBN #978-1-945102-59-2

Printed in the United States of America.

For my granddaughter
Zuri Dior White

"God loves a cheerful giver" **(II Cor. 9:7b).**

Jesse is in the car with his parents, and his mother says, "Jesse, on our way to Abuela's house, let's see how many helpful people we can spot. I like to call these people givers because they give to others through their jobs."

As they pass the hospital, they see a medical doctor, walking to her car.

Pointing to the doctor, Jesse's mother says, "Doctors are givers because when people are sick or hurt, doctors help make the people feel better."

Medical Doctors

After Jesse and his parents pass the hospital, Jesse begins to get comfortable in his seat. Just as he thinks about taking a nap until they reach his grandmother's house, his father points to a car that is next to them as they sit at a red light.

"Hey, son. Do you think police officers are givers?"

Jesse lifts his head and sees two officers sitting in the patrol car. "Yes, Papa. They help keep us safe from bad people who try to hurt us."

Jesse's father nods his head in agreement.

Police Officer

Jesse's mother can see Jesse is a bit tired. She tells him to lean back and close his eyes. Jesse soon falls asleep. But, he doesn't stay that way for long. About ten minutes into his nap, a loud screeching sound startles him. He jumps up in his seat to see what the noise is and from where it is coming. He notices his father has moved their car to the side of the street. Turning his head to look out the window, he sees a large red firetruck racing past them.

"There must be a fire they need to put out," Jesse says before his parents can ask him how a firefighter gives to others.

Firefighters

Soon, Jesse and his family are driving again. From the freeway, Jesse can see his old neighborhood. He remembers when he was in kindergarten. His mother asks, "Was Miss Pam a good teacher, Jesse?"

"Yes, and I really liked her."

"What makes you say she was a good teacher? What did she teach you?"

"She taught me how to write my first sentence and how to add numbers."

"So, would you say teachers are givers?"

"Yes, Mama. Teachers share what they know with us, so we can be smart, too."

"That's right," Jesse's father says.

Teacher

Next, Jesse and his parents pass a cathedral. His father looks at Jesse and asks, "Are there any givers inside there?"

Jesse nods his head and says, "Yes, Papa. The minister is a giver. He gives us the Word of God to help us live right."

"Very good, Jesse. I think you are pretty good at finding givers around town."

Jesse smiles and nods his head.

Minister

"Look, Mama! I see another giver over there."

Jesse's mother turns her head to see who Jesse has spotted this time. She smiles when she sees the postal carrier getting out of his truck to deliver the mail.

"Yes, you are right," she says.

Postal Worker

"Jesse?" his father calls to him in the back seat. "Do you think Tio is a giver?"

"I don't know, Papa," Jesse answers.

"Do you know what he does?"

"Not really, Papa."

"He is in the military, the Army. That means he fights wars when our country is at war with other countries. He gives his life to keep all of us safe."

"But, couldn't he get hurt doing that?" Jesse asks.

"Yes, he can, but he decided it would be worth it to keep others safe. Do you understand that?"

"Yes, Papa," Jesse answers.

Soldier

"Do you see that building with the object that looks like a candy cane?" Jesse's mother asks, just as they turn the corner of Abuela's house.

"Yes, I see it," Jesse says, as he looks out the window.

"That is a barber shop where people cut and style hair. Do you think they are givers?"

"I'm not sure."

"Well, think about all the people who want to look nice when they go to work or to a wedding or another important event. The stylists and barbers help people to look their best."

"So, they are givers," Jesse says, as they move down the street to his grandmother's house.

"What about Abuela, Mama? I think she is a giver too because she gives us all her love, and she makes us good food to eat. I can't wait to see her." Both his parents laugh as they all get out of the car and begin to walk up the steps of Abuela's house.

Hair Stylist

"God loves a cheerful giver" (II Cor. 9:7b).

How can you give to those around you who may need your help today?